No More Fish!

by Dawn McMillan
illustrated by Kate Ashforth

SCHOOL PUBLISHERS

Printed in Mexico

ISBN 10: 0-15-350441-2
ISBN 13: 978-0-15-350441-9

Ordering Options
ISBN 10: 0-15-350332-7 (Grade 2 Below-Level Collection)
ISBN 13: 978-0-15-350332-0 (Grade 2 Below-Level Collection)
ISBN 10: 0-15-357450-X (package of 5)
ISBN 13: 978-0-15-357450-4 (package of 5)

2 3 4 5 6 7 8 9 10   050   15 14 13 12 11 10 09 08 07

"Oh, no. Not more fresh fish!" said Fluffy.

"I must admit that I hate fish," Victor replied.

"I can barely eat fish!" cried Cuddles. "Why do we always get fish for dinner?"

"Maybe our owners think we are sharks in disguise!" laughed Cuddles.

"Very witty," purred Fluffy. "Pet sharks! You are so hilarious!"

4

"Our food problem is getting extremely serious," said Victor. "No more joking around! We must do something!"

"I have a plan," said Fluffy. "Let's not eat the fish anymore. Let's just sit by the cupboard. I know there are some cans of cat food in there. They keep them on hand in case there is no fish to buy."

"Canned cat food!" cried Cuddles. "I'd love to eat that every day!"

Cuddles, Fluffy, and Victor sat by the cupboard and waited.

The next day, Victor said, "Your plan is not working, Fluffy. They are still giving us fish. We must *tell* them what we want!"

8

"Do you mean talk to them?" Fluffy asked.

"Give our secret away?" gasped Cuddles.

"I'm afraid so," said Victor. "Let's talk to the boy. He looks as if he can keep a secret."

That afternoon, the boy came into the kitchen.

"We need to talk to you," Victor said to him quite clearly.

The boy dropped the plate he was
holding and stared at the cats.

"We don't want fresh fish anymore,"
said Cuddles.

"Please may we have canned cat food?"
asked Fluffy.

"I didn't know that cats could talk!" stammered the boy.

"Oh, it's our secret," purred Fluffy. "Now it's your secret, too."

"That's amazing!" exclaimed the boy. "I'll ask Mom to buy only canned cat food instead of fish!"

"Hurray," the cats purred. "No more fish for us!"

Think Critically

1. What problem did the cats have? How did they solve it?

2. What was the most important event in the story?

3. Why did the boy drop the plate?

4. How would you have felt if you had been the boy and the cats had spoken to you?

5. Which cat from the book was your favorite? Why?

 **Social Studies**

Rules for Pet Owners Choose a pet and write a list of three rules for people who own this type of pet. Draw a picture for each rule.

School-Home Connection Talk to a family member about why it is important for people to take good care of their pets. Find a picture of a pet in a book or magazine and talk about how you would care for it.

Word Count: 292